A Thousand Questions for Love and Dating

For Newbies and Experts and Everyone In Between

Fun – Serious – Intimate

Things to ask for dating or for friends

Christopher Eyton

SYNIAD HOUSE

First E-Edition January 2020.

Paperback edition February 2024

 ISBN 978-0-9938273-6-5

Syniad House
B33 - 105 Drummond Street East
Merrickville, Ontario
K0G 1N0

To contact the author, email
christophereyton@gmail.com
Or mail Syniad House.

Cover photo © 2008 Christopher Eyton. "Couple in purgatory", statue in roundabout in Malta

Table of Contents

Introduction – Do's and Don'ts

Welcome and thank you for deciding on **A Thousand Questions for Love and Dating**.

The genesis of this book was a divorce. At no point in life is dating easy. Relationships are hard work but getting started can be the hardest part, figuring out if that person across the table is the right person for you. Figuring out if you want to spend your time with this being or keep looking for someone different. That goes the other direction too. Helping the person you are with figure out if you are someone they should spend their time on.

This book isn't meant to be limited to just couples dating. You can always throw out a few questions for your friends – new or old – to see where they stand on things or what stories they might have to tell that you've never heard before.

Obviously, there are vastly more than a thousand questions you can ask. These are meant to be a cross-section on a number of subjects, both fun or serious, intimate or everyday, philosophical or trivial, and everything in-between. Don't limit yourself.

Starting with **The Basics**, we work down into more personal topics through **Advanced Question Asking** and so on. **Probably Not on The First Date** are questions of a sexual nature. Tread carefully! **Been There, Done That** is for anyone but likely to be of interest to those who have dated before or been in a long-term relationship.

After the heavy lifting of the personal and intimate, there are more materialistic questions starting with **It's a Material World** and exploring appetites in **Food and Drinks**. For the nerds in all of us, there is **Kind of Nerdy**, a bit of fun on some strange subjects. And for those questions that didn't fit in anywhere particularly well, have a look in **Potpourri of Curiosity**.

The point of the book is to get conversations going and to get people to open up. To find out about them and maybe to find out a little more about yourself. If you feel awkward or shy, use the questions to get past the initial moments where you aren't quite sure what to say. Maybe memorize a few questions. Those questions can lead to more and before you know it, hopefully, you are chatting away, past that moment of uncertainty.

Some of the questions may feel similar. It is a matter of exploring a subject from different angles or vantage points. Questions have been sorted by what felt like the logical placement, but some questions can cover a number of themes or thoughts. Don't get too hung up on how they are sorted. The important thing is the question and the answer it draws out.

Here are a few do's and don'ts:

As above, **don't limit yourself**. If you think of something that isn't in this book and it is a good question to ask, then fire away!

Do show discretion. For any question, there is a time or place to ask it. If the person you are with doesn't want to answer a question, don't push it. This especially true with intimate or questions of a sexual nature.

Do remember the answers that are given to your questions. Especially ones of a very personal nature or ones that are important to the person you are talking to. A good idea used by diplomats and other successful individuals: if you are out somewhere and you learn something important but can't write it down right away, write it down as soon as you can, before you go to sleep so you don't forget the details. (Another good rule followed by diplomats for alcohol: when you are out at a social event and don't want to get drunk, drink the first drink, sip the second drink, and hold the third drink.)

Don't laugh at an answer unless it is meant to be funny. You don't want to be disrespected and other people don't want to be either. As you get to know someone, this gets easier to get right.

Do be kind to yourself. Just because you ask thoughtful questions and try to do everything right, doesn't mean that it is going to work out if you are on a date. Sometimes the lives and views of two people are too far apart for it to work out. That doesn't mean you shouldn't try but if it doesn't work out it isn't necessarily anybody's fault. So, be kind to yourself.

Do be honest. You may really like the person you are chatting with and really want them to like you. But if you lie about an answer or a topic, in the long-run it will come back to bite you in the ass – and not in a fun, sort of kinky way.

Do take the time to listen. Enjoy the conversation. Whether it is asking questions or answering them, or just chatting away about this and that, relax, and enjoy interacting and learning. There was an ancient philosopher who offered some good advice: "We have two ears and one mouth so that we can listen twice as much as we speak."

Let me know if you have any comments, concerns, or questions about anything in this book. I especially love learning about typos and then correcting them. On points of grammar, I am willing to listen to suggestions. I can be reached at christophereyton@gmail.com, if you want to write.

Enjoy asking questions. Be brave. Be kind. Be yourself.

The Basics

1: What is your favorite colour?

_____

2: What is your favorite season?

_____

3: What is your favorite sport to watch?

_____

4: What is your favorite sport/activity to participate in?

_____

5: What is your favorite flower?

_____

6: What time of the day and in which city or place where you born?

_____

7: What worries you most about growing older? Why?

_____

8: Given the choice of living anywhere – country, town, city, etc. – where would you want to live? Is there a specific place that you would have in mind?

_____

9: What religion do you consider yourself? Do you follow it much or more of an in-name-only follower?

_____

10: Who is your absolute favorite author?

_____

11. Is there any one philosopher or thinker that you like or follow?

_____

12: Do you like the countryside?

_____

13: What is your all-time favorite store?

_____

14: Who has inspired you the most in your life and why?

_____

15: Do you collect anything? If yes, what and for how long?

_____

16: Do you have any feelings regarding Valentine's Day?

_____

17: What is the most romantic place you can think of?

_____

18: Have you ever broken anything, like an arm or leg? If yes, what happened?

_____

19: What is your favorite wild animal?

_____

20: If you won the lottery – $10 million or more – what is the first you would do after claiming your money and getting it into a bank? What would you do with it in the long term?

_____

21: What book has had the most influence on your life?

_____

22: Who is your absolute favorite artist?

_____

23: When you were little, did you have a favorite tv show?

_____

24: If you could have dinner with any person, alive or dead, fictional or real, who would it be? Why?

_____

25: What is your favorite magazine?

_____

26: What is your favorite musical instrument? If you could study one right now, which would it be?

_____

27: Who is your favorite actor? favorite actress?

_____

28: Is there any sport (i.e., ultimate fighting) that you won't watch? How are you with things like boxing?

_____

29: What is your least favorite colour?

_____

30: You buy a hotdog at a stand on the street: what do you put on it?

_____

31: Have you ever been lost as a child? How did your family react when they found you?

_____

32: Who was your favorite Sesame Street muppet (excluding Cookie Monster)?

_____

33: Musical group/singer you hate more than any other?

_____

34: Do you have a favorite type of tree? If yes, what is it and why?

_____

35: If you had one day to live, how would you spend it? (Money would not be an issue.)

_____

36: If you could have a view of anything from your bedroom window, what would it be of?

_____

37: What is the longest you have ever stayed awake and why?

_____

38: If there was a major war or another pandemic, and this country was threatened/hit, what would you do?

_____

39: If someone played you in a movie or tv show, who do you think would be cast as you?

_____

40: Has there ever been a character from a television show that you really liked and identified with?

_____

41: If you weren't from this country, where would you want to be from? Why?

_____

42: What is your favorite way to exercise?

_____

43: What to you is the perfect temperature?

_____

44: Who is the most famous person you have ever met?

_____

45: Is there a sport that you have never tried that you would like to?

_____

46: How do-it-yourself are you? What things do you prefer to do yourself if you have time?

_____

47: Have you ever been caught up in a natural disaster? (Something bad enough that you feared for your safety.)

_____

48: Is there a sports figure/athlete that you look up to?

_____

49: What would you rate your most important sense?

_____

50: Do you like to dance? If yes, what is your favorite type of dance?

_____

51: What is the sickest you have ever been?

_____

52: What is your favorite news source? (TV, radio, magazines, Internet etc.)

_____

53: Have you ever been hypnotized?

_____

54: Have you ever hunted or been fishing?

_____

55: How do you feel about the different days of the week and why?

_____

56: How much do think is the ideal amount of sleep?

_____

57: Would you take a cooking class as part of a date?

_____

58: How exacting are you about recycling? Do you ever say "forget it" and not bother?

_____

59: How do you feel about trees?

_____

60: Are you comfortable ignoring a call when your phone rings? What is the longest period you have gone without your phone?

_____

61: Is there a song you used to love that you hate now? If yes, why?

_____

62: Do you have a favorite fairy tale or children's story?

_____

63: What band do you love the most? Hate the most?

_____

64: When you write, are you left-handed or right-handed?

_____

65: Do you have a favorite eye colour? Hair colour?

_____

66: Do you work better with music on or if there is silence?

_____

67: If you made an embarrassing mistake – like calling someone by the wrong name – how would you handle it?

_____

68: Do you like swimming?

_____

69: What time of day is your favorite time?

_____

70: What age would you like to live to and why?

_____

71: What is the coldest you have ever been? The hottest?

_____

72: If you found a wallet with cash and credit cards, what effort would you go to in trying to find the rightful owner?

_____

73: What, for you, is the strangest name someone that you met had?

_____

74: Have you ever laughed so hard as you were drinking something that it came out your nose?

_____

75: Have you ever been lost as an adult? If yes, how did you find your way?

76: Do you have to talk to someone regularly to consider them a friend? If you don't talk to a friend for years – for instance, they moved away – would you still consider them a friend?

77: What is the hardest thing you have ever had to do?

78: What is the nicest thing anyone has ever said to you?

79: Do you believe in the supernatural?

80: What activity is really boring to you?

81: Have you ever entered a talent contest? How did you do?

82: Who is the smartest person you have ever met or known?

83: Do you enjoy word games, like scrabble, crosswords etc.?

84: Can you sit in silence with a friend for a long time and not feel uncomfortable?

_____

85: Do you like to buy lottery tickets?

_____

86: Have you ever wanted to create something, like a painting or a book or a song? If you haven't been able to yet, what is holding you back?

_____

87: Which are better pets, dogs or cats or neither? If neither, what is the best type of pet?

_____

88: Going to school, how did/do you get there?

_____

89: What are you superstitious about, if anything?

_____

90: Do you like winter? If yes, what is your favorite part of it?

_____

91: What is worse, to be boring or to be overdramatic?

_____

92: What do you consider to be the best thing about this country? What do you feel is the worst thing?

_____

93: You are lost in the woods and the sun is setting. It is chilly but you won't freeze to death. You have no cell phone service. What would you do?

_____

94: If you had an assignment or project due the next day, would you stay up as late as needed to finish it or would you get to bed early and wake up early to finish it?

_____

95: What is your horoscope sign? Your Chinese horoscope sign? How do you feel about astrology?

_____

96: Is there anything that drives you nuts if it isn't done properly?

_____

97: Have you ever been in a car accident? If yes, what happened?

_____

98: If you wrote a book, what would it be about?

_____

99: How important to you is it for the person you are seeing to share your interests?

_____

100: What is the worst idea you have ever heard of?

_____

101: Have you ever won anything in a lottery or a draw or a contest?

_____

102: What do you think of meditation?

_____

103: Is there something you encounter regularly that you have wondered why it is the way it is?

_____

104: Do you think of yourself as an optimist or a pessimist?

_____

105: What is one word that people who know you would use to describe you?

_____

106: What type of art do you like to have where you live, if any?

_____

107: What qualities make the perfect partner for you?

_____

108: For you, what do you think the key to happiness in life is?

_____

109: How do you feel about recycling: saving the planet or a waste of time?

_____

110: Has your phone ever died at a really embarrassing or awkward moment?

___

111: What are three things that really matter to you?

___

112: What is the longest time you have ever dated or been a partner with someone?

___

113: What would make you move to another city? Another country?

___

114: Were you ever required to study Shakespeare in school? If yes, did you find it fun and enlightening or torturous and incomprehensible?

___

115: When you were young did you have a favorite nursery rhyme, riddle, or joke?

___

116: You hear on the news that a big storm is coming: do you hurry to the store and stock up on supplies or assume it won't be too bad – because they always exaggerate – and just plan on riding it out?

___

117: Does education matter to you?

___

118: Who is the greatest hero of all time?

_____

119: Have you ever had your palm read or fortune told? If yes, did you find any of it come true or was it comically wrong?

_____

120: Is there any type of animal that you would like to see that you haven't?

_____

121: Do you know any poems or songs by heart? If yes, which ones?

_____

122: How has your taste in music changed over the years?

_____

123: What was the first concert you ever went to?

_____

Advanced Question Asking

124: What is the wildest thing you have ever done?

_____

125: Absolute, all-time favorite song?

_____

126: Worst subject in high school? What mark did you usually get?

_____

127: Best subject in high school? What mark did you usually get?

_____

128: Who was your favorite teacher and from what grade?

_____

129: Is there a person in history that you admire?

_____

130: Do you believe in ghosts? Do you think you have ever seen one? If yes, where?

_____

131: Have you ever seen a dead body or somebody die?

_____

132: What is your favorite card game?

_____

133: Do you believe in a god? If yes, how do you imagine him, her, it, them? If no, when did you decide you didn't?

134: Have you ever had to speak in public? If yes, how did it go?

135: What is your favorite style of architecture? Do you have one or is it more case by case?

136: Do you thinking drawing and art in general is something you would like to do? What is your favorite style?

137: If you could learn a new skill – anything – what would it be?

138: Have you ever been to a circus? If yes, did you like it? If no, would you like to go to one?

139: Do you have a favorite bird? If yes, which type?

140: What celebrity or personality did you have a crush on as a youngster? Why? Or if none, why not?

141: Have you ever won a trophy? If yes, what for? What personal achievement are you most proud of?

_____

142: To what extent would you go to help a total stranger?

_____

143: You are on a deserted isle with plenty of food, water, supplies etc., but no way off and you're stuck there no matter what. You are able to get three things. What three things would you want?

_____

144: Who is your oldest (longest known) friend that you are still stay in touch with? How did you meet them?

_____

145: When you get sick are you the sort of person that wants to be pampered and taken care of or the sort that simply wants to be left alone?

_____

146: What is the most spontaneous things you have ever done?

_____

147: If you ever changed religion, which would you choose and why?

_____

148: Who is your favorite saint – if you have one – and why?

_____

149: If there was a war, and they started to draft people to fight, would you let your children be drafted? If no, what would you do?

_____

150: If you had to give something up for Lent – or for a short period for some other religious or personal reason -- what would it be?

_____

151: Have you ever fired a gun or used a bow and arrow? If yes, when?

_____

152: If you could choose now how you died many years from now, from natural causes, how would you like to go?

_____

153: Do you sunburn easily? When did you get your worst sunburn?

_____

154: Has there ever been a book or movie or show that changed the direction of your life?

_____

155: Who was your first love/crush?

_____

156: What is one thing would you like to do before you die, the one thing that is at the top of your bucket list?

_____

157: Have you ever had your appendix or tonsils removed?

_____

158: What would your perfect day consist of?

_____

159: What do you think is the sexiest musical instrument?

_____

160: If someone wanted to do something romantic for you, what you consider to be the most romantic thing possible?

_____

161: Do you have a favorite hymn or sacred song or verse?

_____

162: What is the best practical joke you have ever played?

_____

163: What is the most offensive thing someone could say to you? (Comment, word, etc. – you choose)

_____

164: What are your complete feelings on fur?

_____

165: Which do you think is truer – and why – that love is grown or that love is discovered?

___

166: What is the most surprised you have ever been in your life?

___

167: If you met a girlfriend or boyfriend for an evening out and they arrived wearing something hideously ugly (so ugly people were staring and laughing behind their back), would you say anything?

___

168: What is the song you consider the most romantic that you have ever heard?

___

169: If there is anything you would change about me (hair, clothes, etc.), what would it be?

___

170: What do you want for your next birthday?

___

171: Do you like to play golf? If yes, what type of player are you? What was your best score ever and where did you get it?

___

172: Where is your favorite quiet place for when you need to get away from it all?

___

173: Is there a store that you used to go to that you don't now and miss?

_____

174: If you are out with a group of friends, do you prefer a square/rectangular table or a round one?

_____

175: If you saw someone in distress on the street, and there was no danger to yourself, would you help them?

_____

176: favorite name, boy or girl or other?

_____

177: Have you ever been on a jury or involved in a criminal case?

_____

178: If someone you knew was unjustly convicted and broke out of jail, would you help them if they asked?

_____

179: Do you worry about other people's feelings?

_____

180: Have you ever been ill with something serious or dangerous, like meningitis or pneumonia?

_____

181: What do you usually first notice about someone, even before either of you have said a word?

_____

182: When you were younger, who was your best friend? Are you still friends with them?

___

183: Have you ever accidently insulted someone?

___

184: Do you like to lie on your back on a blanket in a field on a clear summer night and stare at the stars?

___

185: What was the weirdest thing you did as a child?

___

186: Do you support a particular political party? If yes, why?

___

187: Have you ever taken part in any type of protest?

___

188: Have you ever talked yourself out of trouble, like a speeding ticket or school suspension?

___

189: Who, if any, is your role model in life?

___

190: What event that you went to did you expect to be awful but it was actually good and enjoyable?

___

191: If a friend of yours said something offensive or racist, how would you react?

___

192: Does religion matter to you?

_____

193: Revenge, a dish best served cold OR turn the other cheek and forgive. Which would you most likely choose?

_____

194: Of all your senses – sight, touch, hearing, smell, taste – which is your strongest? Which is your weakest?

_____

195: How would you describe the way you dress? Why have you decided to dress that way?

_____

196: A friend makes a horrible fashion or style choice: do you tell them the truth if they ask your opinion?

_____

197: Have you ever tried to pick up or date someone who doesn't speak your language?

_____

198: Who was your all-time favorite friend in school, any year?

_____

199: If someone embarrasses you by accident, do you get angry or do you just try and be stoic about it and pretend it didn't happen?

_____

200: Have you ever won an award or been recognized for some act?

_____

201: Have you ever been caught staring at someone when you thought they weren't looking? How did they react?

_____

202: Hugs or kisses, which do you prefer when saying good-bye to someone?

_____

203: What is the strangest or most unexpected place you have fallen asleep?

_____

204: You and someone you are dating break up on decent terms: do you ghost them?

_____

205: What is the most selfish thing you have ever done? Least selfish?

_____

206: Have you ever laughed at an inappropriate moment?

_____

207: If you aren't feeling well, do you like it when someone comforts you and helps you or do you prefer to be left alone?

_____

208: What makes you happiest each day?

_____

209: What is the shortest date you have been on?
(Hopefully not this one.)

_____

210: Have you ever voted for someone and wished in
hindsight you never had?

_____

211: You are seeing someone you really like and they get
you to watch their favorite movie. You don't really like it
much. Do you pretend that you did or tell them the
truth?

_____

212: Could you live with someone that voted for a different political party than you and insisted on putting a sign
out in support? (Assumes they would not be opposed to
you putting a sign out in support of your choice.)

_____

213: Is there a conspiracy theory that you suspect just
might be true?

_____

214: Have you ever let someone buy you a drink even
though you thought you weren't interested but changed
you mind after talking to them?

_____

215: Exercise: a healthy evil or the best moment of my day?

216: If you go to a religious ceremony – regular service, wedding, funeral, whatever you think of – what is the part you enjoy the most?

217: Do you view life as deadly serious or something to be enjoyed to the most?

218: What is the strangest date you have ever been on?

219: What is the longest you have gone without speaking to another human being?

220: Long, hot shower or soaking in a warm tub, which would you prefer? What if you invited someone to join you in the shower or tub?

221: What do you do if someone you are with is talking too much? Do you suffer in annoyed silence or make them know that you would a appreciate a chance to speak or a little silence?

222: When you overhear people speaking a language you don't understand, how does it make you feel?

223: How old were you when you first had beer or alcohol without your parents' knowledge?

_____

224: What is the scariest thing you have ever seen?

_____

225: If a war broke out and there was fighting near you, would you attempt to flee or would you join the side you supported, assuming there is one?

_____

226: What is the most offensive thing you have ever heard someone say?

_____

227: What is the kindest thing you have ever heard someone say? (It doesn't have to have been said to you.)

_____

228: What do you do when you first wake up? Is it different depending on the day of the week?

_____

229: What animal do you consider to be your spirit guide?

_____

230: If you had a child now, what name would you choose if it is a boy? What about for a girl?

_____

231: Have you ever been forced to sleep in the street or outside because you had no place to stay?

_____

232: What is the angriest you have ever been with someone?

_____

233: How do you feel when an Amber Alert for a missing child sounds in the middle of the night, waking you up?

_____

234: What is the best surprise gift you have ever received?

_____

235: Do you always feel the need to win in any type of competition?

_____

236: What song(s) do you like to sing when you are alone?

_____

237: If you hear a baby crying – and it isn't yours – what do think and do?

_____

238: How can I miss you if you don't go away? – in other words, how much time do you like to spend with the person you are involved with and how much time apart?

_____

239: Have you ever bought something you didn't want only so you could talk to the person selling it?

_____

240: What is your attitude towards strangers?

_____

241: If you found out the person you are seeing had a physical abnormality – such as some webbed toes – would you keep seeing them?

_____

242: Same sex marriage: just not right or same sex couples should suffer like the everyone else?

_____

243: What do you most disapprove of?

_____

244: Would you have a long-distance relationship if you knew that the two of you would live closer together not too far in the future?

_____

245: Have you ever purposely given someone the wrong phone number or email address?

_____

246: Is there someone in your past that you wish you could have continued your relationship with?

_____

247: You are going to be a first-time parent with the baby about to be born any day. Would you want the first born to be a boy or girl?

248: Have you ever hallucinated?

249: Did/do you belong to any cliques in high school? If yes, which one?

250: If someone is sitting near your speaking loudly on a cellphone, would you ask them to lower their voice or go somewhere else to talk?

251: Have you ever ended a friendship because of a political argument?

252: If you are single, do you not worry about it or do you immediately try to find someone new?

253: If someone you knew became homeless – because of a fire or natural disaster – how much would you be willing to help them? What if it was because they mismanaged their personal affairs?

254: Would prefer to be in poor health but have all the money you need or be in excellent health but be in poor shape financially (with no likelihood of things improving)?

_____

255: What is the greatest waste of time?

_____

256: What commonly held view in society do you think should change?

_____

257: Do you think of yourself as open-minded?

_____

258: Have you ever had a bad neighbour?

_____

259: Headphones in public: anti-social and a sign of the breakdown of civil society or a quiet, personal oasis wherever you are?

_____

260: Is forgiveness divine or foolish?

_____

261: What is the dumbest/strangest thing you ever heard of that turned out to be true?

_____

262: Is true love real or just a convenient plot point of movies and books?

_____

263: What is the most romantic marriage proposal you have ever heard of? What is the most ridiculous?

_____

264: Have you ever farted at a bad moment? If yes, how did you handle it?

_____

265: Have you ever had a relative or friend die in a war?

_____

266: Is there a trend or big thing in the news right now that you don't get why it's getting the attention it's getting?

_____

267: How dependent are you on your cellphone? What would you do if you lost it?

_____

Now We're Getting Personal

268: What clothing sizes do you wear?

_____

269: What feature about yourself (physical) do you like the least?

_____

270: What feature about yourself do you like the most?

_____

271: Have you ever stolen anything? If yes, what?

_____

272: What was the scariest thing to ever happen to you?

_____

273: Have you ever cone something good but not told anyone about it? If yes, can you tell me?

_____

274: What is the meanest thing you have ever done?

_____

275: What is the nicest thing you have ever done?

_____

276: What term of endearment (such as: darling, love, babe) do you consider the most romantic?

_____

277: What part of my body do you like the most? What would you like to see improved?

_____

278: When you were little, what did you want to be when you grew up?

_____

279: Have you ever taken illegal drugs? If yes, what and how old were you?

_____

280: If somebody made you breakfast and served it to you in bed, what would you consider the perfect breakfast?

_____

281: What is the strangest thing you are, or have been, subscribed to on the Internet, for example websites, blogs, e-newsletters etc.?

_____

282: Have you ever been arrested for anything? Or charged with anything, even a speeding ticket? In any country?

_____

283: Is there anything worth dying for? Why or why not?

_____

284: You are in an accident that leaves you completely paralyzed. Would you want to continue that way in the hope that someday you can have your injuries healed or would you prefer to die?

_____

285: Do you have a favorite Valentine's memory, including childhood?

_____

286: What was the worst date you ever went on and why?

_____

287: Would you ever stay at a nudist colony or resort?

_____

288: Have you ever been in a physical fight? If yes, what happened?

_____

289: What blood type are you?

_____

290: If you were cremated after you die, would you like some sort of memorial or ashes just scattered over a lake or something like that?

_____

291: If the person you love couldn't sleep, would you prefer that they stay in bed with you and maybe wake you by being restless or for them to quietly get up so as not to disturb you, except you would wake up and they aren't there?

_____

292: What do you consider your best trait to be? Your worst?

_____

293: Did you suffer from acne as a teenager? What was your greatest fear as a teenager?

_____

294: Do you believe in an afterlife?

_____

295: Do you believe love at first sight (first word?) is possible?

_____

296: What have you never done that you would like to do?

_____

297: Is there something you have tried/done before with someone else that you would like to do with me but have been hesitant?

_____

298: Do crowds and small places bother you? If yes, is there particular reason?

_____

299: Are you ever scared of the dark?

_____

300: Have you ever had a one-night stand, the sort where you never see the person again? How did you feel about it, if yes?

_____

301: Has there ever been something, or a situation, that turned you on when you least expected it?

_____

302: Who is your worst enemy? Why?

_____

303: What was the craziest/wildest dare or bet that you have ever taken?

_____

304: Have you ever been robbed or mugged? This includes your home or a business being broken into. If yes, what happened?

_____

305: If you were desperate for money and someone offered you a huge sum of money – enough it that would solve all your money problems for the rest of your life – to have sex them, would you? (Assumes no one outside the two of you would ever know.) Would it make a difference if it was a man or a woman?

_____

306: What is the most tired you have ever been? Have you ever fallen asleep while having sex?

307: What is the worst or most embarrassing thing you have ever been caught doing?

308: What do think is the best way to keep things "fresh" and exciting in a relationship? If you felt your relationship was in a rut, would you tell your partner or wait for them to say something?

309: When you set your eyes on your loved one for the first time in a while, what do you want to do more than anything else?

310: If you ever had a serious addiction to something, what do you think it would be?

311: Where would you like to go/do for your next birthday?

312: Under what conditions would you take prescription drugs? For physical? For mental? Under what circumstances would you say no even if a doctor prescribed them?

313: Which political party or parties have you supported in the past, if any?

_____

314: When you see me, how do you feel, what is your reaction?

_____

315: What is the most dangerous thing you have ever done?

_____

316: Have you ever gotten so drunk you passed out?

_____

317: Has there ever been something that happened or that your partner did while having sex that made you start laughing (or want to)?

_____

318: If someone of the opposite sex flirted with you, would you tell your partner? In the reverse situation, would you want your partner to tell you?

_____

319: What would embarrass you more than anything else?

_____

320: Have you ever been stalked?

_____

321: What is the shortest time you have waited before having sex with someone after you met them? What were the circumstances?

322: Have you ever had a friend who was supposedly straight who suddenly came out of the closet?

323: Do you have any biases towards any type of individual, such as a suburban mom or hipsters?

324: If you had a friend who wanted to participate in a Gay Pride parade and wanted you to march with them – as friendly support – would you?

325: What is the most you have ever weighed? The least?

326: After a long life and happy life, passing away quietly in your sleep, would you want to be buried, cremated, or donated to science?

327: Has anyone ever made you cry? If yes, why?

328: Have you ever punched or hit someone? If yes, why?

329: Would you ever want children, if you don't have them already? If yes, how many?

_____

330: Would you ever want to have a DNA test done to find out your genetic history?

_____

331: What has been the most stressful moment in your life?

_____

332: What has been the happiest moment or memory in your life?

_____

333: What thing in your life do you most regret and wish you could change?

_____

334: What is your happiest memory from your child-hood?

_____

335: Do you like sleeping on the left side of the bed or the right side of the bed, if you have a choice?

_____

336: What was the most painful thing you ever experi-enced?

_____

337: Have you ever had to call emergency services, such as ambulance or police? If yes, why?

_____

338: Have you ever felt paranoid or extreme anxiety? If yes, why?

_____

339: What is the longest you have ever gone without washing or having a shower or bath?

_____

340: If you ever swear, what do you usually say or what words come out of your mouth?

_____

341: Do you, or have you ever, smoked cigarettes? If you still do, have you ever tried to quit or would you want to?

_____

342: Have you ever told a big lie that you were surprised no one realized it wasn't true?

_____

343: Have you ever lied for someone?

_____

344: What are you scared of losing in your life?

_____

345: Have you ever knowingly cheated on your taxes?

_____

346: There was someone you wronged or treated badly when you were younger, but they have moved away. If they were suddenly right here in front of you now, what would you say to them?

_____

347: What are you most comfortable wearing to bed, pajamas, underwear or nothing at all?

_____

348: Do you have, or have you had, an email account that no one knows about? If yes, what is it for?

_____

349: What is a huge turnoff physically that would make you uninterested in someone?

_____

350: Have you ever cheated on a test?

_____

351: Have you ever broken up with someone for a shallow reason?

_____

352: Is there is anything very kind or thoughtful that you did anonymously and haven't ever told anyone about later?

_____

353: Have you ever shoplifted, either on purpose or by accident?

_____

354: Do you like to cuddle up to someone when you are falling asleep or have them cuddle up to you or do you need your own space?

_____

355: Have you ever ended up dating more than one person at the same time ? If yes, how did you handle it?

_____

356: Have you ever passed out or fainted?

_____

357: If you got a tattoo, what would it be of and where would you put it?

_____

358: Have you ever told someone who wasn't a family member that you love them?

_____

359: Have you ever loved someone and lost them?

_____

360: When you look at yourself in the mirror, how do you feel?

_____

361: What has been the best day of your life so far?

_____

362: What has been the worst day of your life?

_____

363: Have you ever woken up and had no idea where you were?

_____

364: Do you have any phobias, such as fear of heights?

_____

365: When you support a political party, do you support it because of its policies or its leader?

_____

366: Are you content with the way you are or is there something you would like to change?

_____

367: On abortion, would you describe yourself as pro-life or pro-choice? (Only ask this one if you are comfortable and open with each other or if you want your time to-gether to end quickly.)

_____

368: Would you ever donate sperm or eggs to a friend so they could have a child, no strings attached for you? What about a stranger who offered to buy them?

_____

369: When do think it's okay to lie?

_____

370: Would you ever have plastic surgery? If yes, what would you change?

_____

371: Do you snore or talk in your sleep? Do you ever sleepwalk?

_____

372: If love is as love does, how do you like to show somebody that you love them?

_____

373: You go out with someone and really enjoy their company. At the end of the evening, they quietly tell you that they had a sex change earlier in their life. Do you keep seeing them or never speak to them again?

_____

374: Is there any ethnic group or race that you don't like or don't trust? If yes, why? If yes, what could get you to change your mind?

_____

375: Have you ever followed a stranger? If yes, why? Have you ever been followed by a stranger?

_____

376: Have you ever been to any type of therapy?

_____

377: Have you ever been to a nude beach? If yes, did you get fully naked? How did you feel about it?

_____

378: What is the greatest injustice that has ever befallen you? Were you able to get justice eventually?

_____

379: Have you ever been threatened or have threatened somebody, i.e., told someone they would be fired if they were ever late again?

380: Have you ever had serious depression? If yes, what caused it?

381: If you found out the person you love wasn't happy in the relationship, what would you do to try and fix it? What if it couldn't be fixed?

382: Would you date someone with a criminal record? What would you do if they hid it from you and you found out later?

383: Would you ever submit to a lie-detector test to prove you were telling the truth about something?

384: Do you believe you should know everything about your partner (and vice versa) or should you have some secrets you keep from each other?

385: Have you ever tried to sneak into someplace you weren't allowed? If yes, why and what happened?

386: Do you pay attention to your surroundings or are you more likely to daydream and be oblivious?

___

387: If you have been involved with someone for awhile, would you ever help groom them if they asked? For instance, by cutting the hair on the back of their neck or trimming their toenails.

___

388: Have you ever sent a text message, photo, or email that you wish you could get back and erase? What happened after it was sent?

___

389: What is the longest period of time you have ever had to stay in a hospital?

___

390: Why have you left someone?

___

391: Have you ever been bullied? Has the person responsible ever tried to apologize or acknowledge what they did?

___

392: Have you ever bullied someone? Have you ever apologized to the person you bullied or tried to make it up to them for it?

___

393: When have you ever been the most terrified? How did you get past it?

_____

394: Do you have someone that you consider a lifelong friend? A lifelong enemy?

_____

395: Who are you closer to, your mother or your father?

_____

396: Is there someone in your past that you wish you could get back together with?

_____

397: Who was your first romantic kiss with?

_____

398: Do you ever suffer from insomnia?

_____

399: Do you ever feel lonely?

_____

Been There, Done That

400: If you ever went back for more education, what would you study? Would it be something to further your career or for the enhancement of your enjoyment of life (knowledge for the sake of knowledge)?

401: Other the end of the scale, you are old and ready to retire: where would you like to retire to and what would you like to do when you retire?

402: If you decided to learn another language, what would it be?

403: If you ever got married again, and could hold the ceremony anywhere you wanted, where would you hold it?

404: If there was one thing or moment you could change in your life, what would it be and why?

405: Have you ever had to fire anybody? If yes, why?

406: What have you always wanted to learn but have never had the chance?

407: When your kids are all older (past university), do you believe in keeping a place for them (extra rooms) in our home or are you more of the attitude that once they have flown the nest, they have flown the nest?

_____

408: What is your greatest hope for each of your children?

_____

409: What do you think you would like to do as a hobby or pastime when you are retired to keep yourself busy?

_____

410: Would you ever want your own business?

_____

411: Does anything scare you about growing older?

_____

412: Do you still get along with your ex?

_____

413: Are you happy with how old you are now?

_____

414: How has your life turned out differently so far than what you expected when you were 18?

_____

415: Is there anyone that you were once close to that you are now estranged from? If yes, what happened? Would you ever want to fix the rift?

_____

416: What sound brings back happy memories? Sad memories?

___

417: Have you ever picked up or dated someone you met at a completely unexpected place, like a funeral or a car wash?

___

418: Have you ever been afraid you might die?

___

419: Which of your childhood friends changed in a way you didn't expect as they got older? How did they change?

___

420: What do you like best about growing older so far?

___

421: What do you like the least about growing older so far?

___

422: If you could choose any age to be, what would it be and why?

___

423: You are out with someone you have been seeing for awhile: who pays for what? What about if you are just doing chores and other everyday things you both benefit from?

___

424: What experience do you wish you could scrub from your life? If you could, how would it change the course of your life from that point?

_____

425: What is your primary goal in life at this point of time? How has it changed over the years?

_____

426: Who did you want to meet when you were younger? Did you ever try to meet them or succeed in meeting them?

_____

427: Is there anything you used to worry about that you don't anymore?

_____

428: What is better, to be a favorite uncle or aunt or to be a grandmother or grandfather?

_____

429: How old were you when you moved out and went on your own for the first time?

_____

430: What would you consider to be good reasons to divorce a spouse?

_____

431: What is something you do now that you couldn't have imagined you would be doing when you were younger?

_____

432: You are married, and you find out your partner cheated on you. You decide to stay in the marriage. Do you tell everyone you know what they did, or do you keep it to yourself?

_____

433: What would you do if you found out your partner was mentally ill but refused to recognize it?

_____

434: What would be worse for you: to lose your mind because of dementia but your body is healthy or to be locked in a paralyzed body with a healthy mind?

_____

435: How old do you think is too old to try something new?

_____

436: You are about to become a proud parent or grand-parent. Do you want to know the sex of the baby before it is born?

_____

437: Do you believe in growing old gracefully or that growing older is a cage fight and you're going to win?

_____

438: Has your perception of time changed as you have gotten older?

_____

439: Is there something you loved doing – like playing a sport – that you had to give because of getting older?

_____

440: Is it ever too late – before you die – to start exercising, eating better, and getting more fit in general?

_____

441: Your partner – whom you loved completely – passes away. Do you start to date again after waiting a certain amount of time or stay single the rest of your life? If you start seeing others again, how long would you wait?

_____

All About Family and Friends

442: If you were in trouble, who would you turn to, your mother or your father?

_____

443: If you have siblings or a sibling, do you get along with them? If you have more than one, do you have a favorite?

_____

444: What was your first pet? What was his/her name and was it just yours or the whole family's?

_____

445: Would you ever adopt a child?

_____

446: Outside of your siblings (and their spouses) and parents, do you have any other relatives you're close to?

_____

447: How far would you go to please a loved one?

_____

448: What sort of child did most people consider you when you were little?

_____

449: What is your first memory?

_____

450: How long do members of your family usually live? (Approximately.)

_____

451: If you decided to change your name, what would you change it to?

_____

452: How many pets have you had in your life? Can you remember them all?

_____

453: If you lost everything – family, friends, possessions, everything – what would you do?

_____

454: Were you ever spanked as a child?

_____

455: If someone hurt, harmed, or killed someone you love, would you take action yourself after the fact or leave it to the justice system?

_____

456: Do you have any holiday traditions in your family? How do you mark them?

_____

457: Do you have any relatives that you would prefer not to have anything to do with?

_____

458: If one of your kids was going to marry someone you thought was bad for them, would you try and stop the marriage?

459: If you could learn to sing and play one song perfectly, that you could perform in front of family and friends, what would it be?

460: If you had to sacrifice a family member (and you can't sacrifice yourself) to save all your other family members, who would you sacrifice?

461: What would you do if one of your kids ever joined a gang, for instance, Hell's Angels?

462: Which relative would you most enjoy being with for a day IF you could only do what they want to do? Why?

463: Have you ever contemplated running away from home?

464: Have you ever had a personal servant or nanny or regular babysitter? If yes, do you stay in touch with them?

465: What is your favorite cottage memory?

_____

466: Who has been the most important influence in your life outside of your family?

_____

467: Is there one adult who wasn't a relative that sticks out in your mind from your childhood? If yes, why?

_____

468: Have you ever had to care for someone who was an invalid?

_____

469: What is the strangest pet you have ever had?

_____

470: If someone close to you was very ill for awhile, would you help take care of them?

_____

471: Who was the most important person in your life when you were growing up?

_____

472: What was the funniest thing you did as a child?

_____

473: For big holidays, do you like to get together with friends and/or family?

_____

474: Is there anyone you miss that you haven't seen for a long time?

_____

475: Is there anyone in your family that no one really talks about but everyone is aware of?

_____

476: Do you like to celebrate your birthday or do you prefer people not to notice it?

_____

477: What are your favorite and least favorite holidays?

_____

478: Do you think children should be spanked if they misbehave?

_____

479: Have you ever seen a baby being born?

_____

480: How old were you found out that babies come from inside mothers?

_____

481: Who are you closest to in your family? If you don't have any family, who were you closest to growing up?

_____

482: If someone is having children, do you think it is better to have a son or a daughter first? Why?

_____

483: Would you ever date or marry someone who was from a different religion than you? Different country? Different ethnic background?

_____

484: Do you play jokes on friends or family?

_____

485: How old were you before you were allowed to walk /travel to school by yourself?

_____

486: What is the most trouble you have ever gotten into at home? At school? At work?

_____

487: Do you have a nickname that family/friends call you? If yes, how did you get the nickname and how do you feel about it?

_____

488: What single word would best describe your childhood?

_____

489: Did you have a favorite toy or stuffed animal when you were young?

_____

490: Is there an illness or disease that seems to afflict members of your family?

_____

491: If you have children or want them: would you want each child to be wealthy or famous or happy?

___

492: You arrive home early to find a relative (child, sibling, parent etc.) who lives with you doing something that is harmless but makes you feel uncomfortable. They don't know you are home. Do you say something or quietly slip away and never say anything about it?

___

493: Do you believe you should respect elders? What if they are wrong about something? Do you think you should correct them, even if it publicly embarrasses them?

___

494: Is there any trait from your parents that you worry you inherited that hasn't shown up yet?

___

495: What are your feelings about marriage? Should a couple have a formal religious service or a civil service or live common law?

___

496: What are your feelings about divorce?

___

497: Is there any reason you would disown a child or disavow any other relative?

___

498: Would you ever put a child up for adoption? If yes, under what circumstances?

_____

499: Would you change religions for the person you love?

_____

500: Who in your life has surprised you the most?

_____

501: Is there someone in your family that everyone refers to as an Aunt or Uncle who isn't actually related to you? If yes, how did they become part of your family?

_____

502: What do you think is the strangest holiday?

_____

503: If someone in your family is going to remarry, and you believe their new spouse is only marrying them for their money but you have no real proof, do you say something?

_____

504: If you were choosing a dog, what size would you want, small, medium, or large?

_____

505: Have you ever skipped a wedding or a funeral because you didn't like someone very much?

_____

506: What is the worst wedding you have ever been to? The best?

_____

507: Have you ever crashed an event, like a birthday party or a wedding? What happened?

_____

508: Do you know much about your family tree?

_____

509: How do you feel about blended families? Do you think of yours as one?

_____

510: Do you play favorites with your children/siblings/relatives?

_____

What To Do With Free Time

511: If you could travel anywhere in the world, where would you go? Why?

_____

512: If you could travel to the edge of space on the Virgin Galactic spaceship (www.virgingalactic.com) someday in the future, would you?

_____

513: Have you ever been on a ship cruise? If yes, where and when and did you enjoy it?

_____

514: If you have been on one, where did you go on your honeymoon? Did you like it? If you ever went on another "honeymoon", where do you think you would like to go? Would you prefer to be surprised?

_____

515: Have you been on a trip in a RV or Campervan? If yes, did you like it? Would you do it again?

_____

516: Where would you like to go on your next vacation? If there are children, where do you think the kids would like to go?

_____

517: Do you like roller coasters, amusement parks etc.? If you went to an amusement park, what would your favorite type of ride be?

_____

518: Have you ever been to a bullfight? What do you think of them?

_____

519: Which do you find more romantic, watching a sunset or sunrise with the person you love? Why? Which is better, watching from a mountaintop or a secluded beach by the ocean?

_____

520: Have you ever ridden a motorcycle? If no, do you think you would like to and would you like to drive or be behind as the passenger? If yes, did you enjoy it?

_____

521: What is the most exotic place you have ever been? Would you visit again?

_____

522: What was the best concert you ever went to?

_____

523: How would you describe your ideal vacation?

_____

524: Given the choice and time not being an issue, what is your favorite way to travel, train, car, plane, boat, or someway else?

_____

525: Are there any "thrill" adventures, rides, activities you think you would like to try? (In example, white water rafting.)

_____

526: Would you ever go on a submarine?

_____

527: What was your all-time favorite vacation?

_____

528: If you could live anywhere, what size place (village, town, countryside, city) would you consider ideal?

_____

529: If you could travel in time, is there any particular time and place you would want to live other than this one? Why?

_____

530: If you could live in another country for a short time (at least one year), and it could be any country in the world, which would it be?

_____

531: Have you ever been to summer camp?

_____

532: Would you be willing to go "camping" if it was glamping?

_____

533: Have you ever been on a really long road trip? What road trip do you remember most fondly?

_____

534: What is the worst motel or hotel you have ever stayed in?

_____

535: Have you ever tried to surf (with a board)? Do you think you would like to if you haven't?

_____

536: What is your favorite form of live entertainment, excluding concerts? (Comedy clubs, theatre, etc.)

_____

537: Do you have a favorite hotel?

_____

538: Do you ever get car sickness or motion sickness when you're travelling?

_____

539: Would you ever want to visit the place you were born?

_____

540: Would you ever be willing to cruise along a river in a houseboat if it was a really nice one? What about a converted barge?

_____

541: Is there a famous sight you have always wanted to travel to and see? (In example, the Pyramids).

542: Are there any famous annual or regular events – such as the Running of the Bulls in Spain or Carnival in Brazil – anywhere in the world that you would love to take part in?

543: What is the best tourist attraction (museum, park, site, whatever) that you have ever been too?

544: Which comedian or actor makes you laugh more than any other?

545: Do you have a favorite play?

546: Have you ever slept overnight on a boat or a ship?

547: How do you feel about treehouses?

548: What is your favorite place to visit in your home-town?

549: If you are flying somewhere, what is most important to you, cost or comfort or something else?

550: What is the tackiest tourist thing you have ever done/visited?

551: Where do you consider to be your true home? (What place now or in the place feels most like a home?)

552: What is the farthest north/south/west/east you have ever gone from the place you consider home?

553: Would you ever like to go on a treasure hunt?

554: What is the most unusual place (hotel, house, etc.) that you have stayed overnight in?

555: What sport do you consider the dumbest? Most boring? Why?

556: Do you like to drive in bad weather, such as rain or snow?

557: What is the most money, if any, you have ever gambled or placed on a bet? Did you win or lose?

558: If money was no object, where would you go for a trip or a vacation? What place have you always wanted to visit?

_____

559: Do you like road trips?

_____

560: What country would you never visit and why?

_____

561: Do you like to read a book or watch it as a movie?

_____

562: Did you have a favorite book as a child? If yes, what was it?

_____

563: Do you like to look at maps? Are you good at reading them?

_____

564: What is the worst movie you have ever seen?

_____

565: Do you have a favorite television show? If yes, why do you like it?

_____

566: Have you ever played paintball or an adult tag game like that?

_____

567: Have you ever explored a cave?

___

568: What is your favorite genre of book or story to read?

___

569: If you are on a train or plane, what sort of person would you like to sit beside you if the seat was empty?

___

570: In the place that you live, is there a tourist attraction or famous site that you have never visited?

___

571: What is the scariest movie or show you have ever seen? Most romantic?

___

572: Have you ever cheered for a team that wasn't your hometown team?

___

573: Do you swim or do you find going out in water frightening?

___

574: What is the smallest town or village you have ever visited? Why did you go?

___

575: Do you like zoos?

___

576: How many countries other than your own have you visited in your life? Which was your favorite? Which was your least favorite?

577: If you have your license, do you like to drive or is it just a means of getting around? If you don't have it, would you want to get it?

578: Is there a sports team or musical group/band you are fanatically devoted to? If yes, how long have you liked them and why?

579: What place that you have never been to do you think would be very romantic to visit?

580: Do you like to pick up free reading material, like tourism pamphlets, when it is available or just look everything up on the internet?

581: Do you ever wander around cemeteries and read the gravestones?

582: Which would you prefer to do: visit a famous battlefield or ride a terrifying roller coaster or watch a football game?

583: What is the best festival, if any, that you have ever been to?

_____

584: Do you ever dress up for holidays – like Halloween – or parties? If yes, what was your best costume?

_____

585: Have you ever been in any type of play or live performance?

_____

586: What was your favorite movie as a child? As a teenager? As an adult?

_____

587: What was your favorite tv series as a child? As a teenager? As an adult?

_____

588: Would you go out to sea on a freighter if you had the chance? (Assuming it is free or cheap and takes you to someplace you want to go.)

_____

589: Would you prefer to dress casually and go to a relaxed event or dress up and go to a more formal event, like a charity gala or high-end restaurant?

_____

590: Would you prefer to lie on a towel on a crowded beach by the sea or lie on a blanket in an empty field surrounded by forest?

591: What is the longest road trip you have ever been on? Where did you go?

592: How many places have you lived in your life?

593: Do you enjoy watching classic movies, like Casablanca or Titanic?

594: Is there a movie that you loved as a child that is hard to watch now?

595: What is the best live show or performance – of any type of act – that you have ever seen?

596: You have a flight leaving from a busy airport: do you get there early to check in so you aren't rushed or do you cut it as close as you can for checking in so you aren't wasting time hanging around the airport?

597: Do you like reality shows or lifestyle shows, like home or cooking shows?

598: Do you enjoy a bonfire on a summer night in the country or at a cottage or a beach?

_____

599: Do you like gardens? Do you like gardening?

_____

600: Do you like stand-up comedians?

_____

601: Do you mind taking public transit in cities you know? What about cities you are just visiting for the first time?

_____

Career and Ambitions
and a Bit of Dreaming

602: What was your first job?

_____

603: What lengths would you go to, to be successful? In other words, if you were in a competitive situation, and there were things of questionable morality (but not illegal) that would get you in front, what would you do?

_____

604: What summer jobs did you have growing up?

_____

605: Do you prefer to learn things by trial and error or by being taught by an expert?

_____

606: Do you think you would ever want to own a restaurant or a hotel/b&b or a pub or a winery? If yes, what would your ideal be?

_____

607: If you were given a one-year sabbatical from your job, and money was no object, what would you do with your sabbatical?

_____

608: If someone offered you a role in a tv show or a movie, would you go for it?

_____

609: Would you prefer to be rich or famous? How would you like to get there?

_____

610: If you could learn a circus skill, would you want to?

_____

If yes, what skill would you want to learn?

_____

611: Have you ever built anything? If yes, what was it?

_____

612: Given the choice of living a long, comfortable, sub-urban life in which you are basically happy but completely anonymous or a wild life in which everyone knew your name (in a good way), you are fabulously wealthy, but your life is turbulent with many highs and lows, which would you pick?

_____

613: Being allowed only to choose one of these, which is the most important to you: health, money, or love? Why?

_____

614: What talent or skill do you have that no one suspects?

_____

615: Have you ever entered a contest for something you created, such strawberry jam, for example?

_____

616: Have you ever been fired from a job?

_____

617: What is the worst job you have ever had?

_____

618: What is the best job you ever had?

_____

619: If you could be the first person on another planet, like Mars, but there is a 50% chance you wouldn't make it back, would you go? What if it was 80% chance of not making it back?

_____

620: If you could start you own business or project, and start-up funds weren't an issue, what type of business or project would you start?

_____

621: So far, what do you think of as your greatest achievement or moment in your life?

_____

622: If you could have any job or career in the world, what would it be?

_____

623: What does the word "socialism" mean to you? What about "capitalism"?

_____

624: When you were at school, did you ever join any clubs or teams?

_____

625: Have you ever been forced to study something that seemed like a waste of time then, but you are glad you did now?

_____

626: How are you with public speaking: "fine, it's all good" or "no, I'd prefer to have my nails pulled out"?

_____

627: Are you the grasshopper or the ant? (Would you prefer to live life for the moment or work to ensure your constant wellbeing?)

_____

628: Is there a job you consider to be beneath you?

_____

629: Have you ever fallen for a scam?

_____

630: Would you ever want to own a franchise? If yes, what type?

_____

631: Have you ever kept a job you hated only because you couldn't afford to lose it? How did you eventually get out of it?

_____

632: Have you ever had a role in a movie, tv show, or video, even if only as an extra?

_____

633: Would you ever run for political office? If yes, why?

_____

634: Would you prefer to type a letter on a computer or tablet or write it by hand?

_____

635: Have you ever invented anything or found an unexpected way of solving a problem? (Could be something everyday like keeping the cat off the counter.)

_____

636: Have you ever had a job that you didn't tell your friends or family about?

_____

637: Have you ever belonged to a union or would you be willing to join one if it got you a better job?

_____

638: What are you willing to sacrifice in your life to achieve your goals?

_____

639: When you are at work, would you prefer to have lunch by yourself at a park or with your co-workers at a restaurant?

_____

640: Have you ever dated or seen someone romantically that you work with? How did it work out?

641: What year of school – whether elementary, secondary, or beyond – did you have the most trouble with? What was your best year?

642: Have you ever been unemployed even though you wanted to work?

643: Would you prefer to work a relatively mundane job that wasn't widely respected but paid very well with good benefits or to have work that was unpredictable in pay but brought you attention and respect?

644: Are you willing to take risks that could pay off in a big way even if there is good chance you will publicly fail? What if the reward for succeeding was personal satisfaction but nothing material?

645: Have you ever kept a secret of a co-worker that would have gotten them fired if it was found out?

646: Have you ever suffered from a ransomware attack or virus that screwed up all your work?

647: What you ever walked out of an interview?

___

648: Would you accept a dangerous job if it included significantly more pay?

___

649: Would you join a club/society/fraternity to advance your career even if you didn't total agree with their rules or philosophy?

___

650: If you could star in a movie or tv series, which one would it be and what role would you take?

___

651: You have started a new company or business: what would you call it?

___

652: Taxes: do you see them as necessary to preserve society or a form of legalized theft imposed to pay for things you shouldn't have to pay for?

___

653: Have you ever had a skill or talent that you gave up on that you would like to try again in the future?

___

654: Are billionaires criminals who fixed the system in their favour or deserving of everything they have accumulated? Is there any famous/super rich individual that you think should be in prison?

_____

655: Is there any point in taking part in protests or becoming an activist for a cause?

_____

Probably Not On The First Date

656: Do you like having the palms of your hands and your fingers kissed?

_____

657: What part of your body do you consider your most erogenous?

_____

658: What is your favorite sexual position?

_____

659: Do you ever like to be bitten?

_____

660: Have you ever used a vibrator?

_____

661: Have you ever been tied up and blindfolded on a bed? If yes, did you like it? If no, would you like to try it?

_____

662: Do you like to talk dirty during sex?

_____

663: Have you ever made love in a hammock then fallen asleep under the stars, as the hammock slowly swings?

_____

664: What was the most embarrassing thing that ever happened to you while having sex? (In example, somebody walking in on you.)

_____

665: Do you like getting full body massages (with massage oil) from your partner?

_____

666: Do you prefer to make love with the lights on or off? Candlelight counts as half-way in-between.

_____

667: Have you ever watched your partner play with himself/herself? Did you like it? Have you ever had a partner watch you?

_____

668: What do you consider to be your biggest turn-ons?

_____

669: Is there any part of your body you don't like being touched? If yes, what is it and why?

_____

670: Have you ever made love in a bedroom or room with mirrors or a mirror so you can watch yourself and your partner? If yes, did you like it?

_____

671: Have you ever been skinny-dipping? If yes, what were the circumstances?

_____

672: Do you enjoy giving oral sex?

_____

673: What is the kinkiest thing you ever thought about doing but haven't? If the opportunity presented itself, do you think you would want to actually do it?

_____

674: Have you ever made love on the kitchen table? If no, do you think you would like to?

_____

675: Someone is pouring a liquid on your body and then licking it off. They then kiss you deeply. You can taste the liquid on their tongue and lips. Which would turn you on more, sweet or savory? Is there a specific food (taste) that turns you on more than any other?

_____

676: What position have you fantasized about trying that you have never tried?

_____

677: What movie that you have ever watched has most turned you on? A real movie with a plot not porn.

_____

678: Are you a member of the mile-high club? If not, would you like to join it?

_____

679: Where do you like to be kissed the most? Which kisses drive you wild?

_____

680: Have you ever had your lover drink wine and then slowly let it drip from his mouth into yours as you lay on the bed? If yes, did you like it and do you prefer red or white wine? If no, would you like to try?

_____

681: Do you have any fetishes? If yes, what are they?

_____

682: Have you ever seen someone else having sex? (Live, as opposed to porn or tv) This includes walking in on someone, or a couple getting wild near you, or seeing a sex show? If yes, what were the circumstances?

_____

683: Would you prefer to be woken up with kisses in the morning and make love then or make love in the evening and fall asleep in each other's arms?

_____

684: Sexually speaking, is there anything that you definitely have not wanted to try? If yes, what is it and why?

_____

685: How do you think you would like me to kiss you best?

_____

686: What are your thoughts on erotic movies? Are there times you ever like to watch them?

_____

687: OK, we've kissed already: What do you like me kissing the most: fingertip, nipple, lips? Or somewhere else?

_____

688: How would you feel about going into a sex shop and seeing if there was anything you would like to get?

_____

689: Have you ever gone to work with no panties on? If yes, did you like it?

_____

690: What is the strangest thing you have tried sexually?

_____

691: Wildest sex thing that you have ever done that you would like to repeat again but haven't had a chance to?

_____

692: Ok, you've kissed me: How do I taste?

_____

693: What is your favorite part of me?

_____

694: What position makes you cum harder than any other?

_____

695: When we make love, what would you like me to do differently? (In example, more of, less of, something I don't do now.)

_____

696: What is the strangest/most unusual place you have ever had sex?

_____

697: Do you like to suntan naked?

_____

698: Have you ever surprised a lover? If yes, what did you do? Did you enjoy surprising him/her?

_____

699: Have you ever used any sex toys? If yes, what were they and did you like them?

_____

700: Do you consider yourself as dominant or submissive?

_____

701: Is there part of your body that you would like kissed that has never been kissed before?

_____

702: What is the most orgasms you've had in a short time? What was different?

_____

703: What type of lingerie/underwear do you like to wear most? Is there any type of garment/item you would like to see your partner in?

704: Have you ever made love in a sauna? Would you like to?

705: Has your partner ever tried to get you to take part in a threesome? If yes, how did you handle it?

706: What do you think would be the best way for us to cum together, that is, at the same time? (Note: Wait until you've had sex for this one.)

707: Which do you prefer more and why? Me laying behind you with my arms wrapped around you or me laying in front of you and facing you, with my arms around you?

708: Would you prefer to be kissed from head to toe or from toe to head? How long would you like it to take?

709: Would you ever want to make a sex video if you were sure it would never be found by anyone else?

710: Imagine you made a sex video and it got out into the public so others could see it. How would you feel and what would you do about it?

_____

711: Have you ever had sex in an office/work environment?

_____

712: What gives you your strongest orgasms?

_____

713: What is your favorite type of hug? Describe it!

_____

714: What is the most erotic thing you have ever seen?

_____

715: Have you ever had Brazilian/Manzilian waxing or trimmed the hair around your privates?

_____

716: Do the drapes match the carpet?

_____

717: Have you ever played "Truth or Dare"?

_____

718: What is the dirtiest thing you have ever done?

_____

719: Do you like to talk during sex? Are you noisy?

_____

720: Do you like to French kiss?

_____

721: Do you like to be spanked? What is the kinkiest thing you have ever done?

_____

722: What smell turns you on?

_____

723: What do you think of as your first memorable sexual experience?

_____

724: Have you ever tried a threesome? If not, have you ever been curious to try?

_____

725: What is the longest time you have ever had sex in one stretch?

_____

726: Have you ever been filmed having sex or performing a sexual act? If no, have you ever wanted to try it?

_____

727: Have you ever had sex with someone that didn't speak the same language as you and you didn't speak their language?

_____

728: How old were you when you lost your virginity? Was it a good experience or bad or sort of forgettable?

_____

729: Have you ever played strip poker? If no, would you like to try it someday? If yes, would you like to try again someday and did you win the last time?

730: Have you ever fantasized about a different person when you were having sex with someone?

731: What do you prefer on your lover, a skinny little butt or a big round booty?

732: Have you ever tried anal sex? If no, have you ever been curious about it or too gross to think about?

733: Do you like to make love in the morning or in the evening? Or will anytime of day or night do?

734: Have you ever had sex outdoors or in a public place? If no, have you ever fantasized about it?

735: Are you comfortable going out without a bra?

736: What food do you consider to be the most sensual?

737: Whipped cream or honey or maple syrup?

738: Have you and someone you were with ever both started laughing uncontrollably during sex?

_____

739: Do you like it if your partner has their body completely waxed and all hair removed?

_____

740: How many people have you had sex with, in your life?

_____

741: Have you ever had sex with someone on your first date with them?

_____

742: Is there something that makes you horny that you haven't ever told anyone about?

_____

743: Have you ever had sex in a pool or a hot tub?

_____

744: How long should a couple date before having sex?

_____

745: What are your feelings about sperm?

_____

746: What do you think of open relationships?

_____

747: Have you ever had a sponge bath with hot, foamy water?

_____

748: You and your partner both want sex but only have about 10 minutes before company arrives. Do you go for it?

_____

749: Have you ever had sex with someone you hadn't planned to – such as a close friend – and it didn't change your relationship?

_____

750: If you could kiss someone for hours but not have sex – or do anything else sexual – would you?

_____

751: Have you ever needed a "safe word"? If yes, what was the word you chose?

_____

752: Have you ever given a penis or a vagina a nick-name? If yes, what nickname did you go with?

_____

753: What parts of their body do you like your partner to shave or trim their hair?

_____

754: Have you ever had something or someone turn you on or excite you that surprised you? If yes, what was it and why?

_____

755: Have you ever tried to have sex in every room of your home?

_____

756: Have you ever had sex with someone and never found out their name? Do you regret it or still fantasize about it?

_____

757: Are you ticklish? Do you like to be tickled? If yes, which part of your body?

_____

758: Have you ever danced naked?

_____

For Him, For Her, and Non-binary

759: What is more intimidating, meeting your partner's children – if they have any – or their siblings or parents? (Meeting the young versus meeting the old.)

760: Have you ever had someone interested in you as more than a friend but you just wanted to be friends? How did you handle it?

761: What do you think is the perfect breast size?

762: When you look at me, is there anyone I remind you of?

763: Who was the worst partner you ever had?

764: What is your view of women as managers and political leaders?

765: What was the wildest stag or party you have been to?

766: What are your feelings about women in sports? Are there any you watch? How do you feel about trans-women in sports?

___

767: What is your favorite part of a woman's body?

___

768: Have you ever been asked out by a woman instead of you asking her out? How did you respond?

___

769: If you were having a baby with someone, would you want to be with her while she gave birth?

___

770: How do you feel about natural processes for women, such as pregnancy, birth, menstruation, or breast feeding?

___

771: Which do you think is harder, having children by caesarian or by natural means?

___

772: In public, do you like your partner to be affectionate and hold you close or to be a little more distant but still attentive? What do you consider to be "too much" in public?

___

773: Who was the worst friend you ever had and why?

___

774: Which muscles of mine (specifically) would like to see me work on?

_____

775: How do you like your partner's hair to be cut? Wild, neat, or bald/shaved? Something else?

_____

776: Were you ever a girl guide/scout or anything like that? If yes, did you like it?

_____

777: If you see some good-looking guy walking down the street toward you what do you notice first about him?

_____

778: If you see an attractive woman walking down the street toward you what do you notice first about her?

_____

779: What is the most memorable girls'/boys' night out or stagette/stag you have ever been to and why?

_____

780: If you go to a fitness club, would you prefer one that is women-only or mixed?

_____

781: What do you think is the perfect penis size?

_____

782: Do you think it is better for a man to be circumcised or uncircumcised? Or does it make no difference?

_____

783: Have you ever had multiple orgasms? If yes, was there anything in particular that brought you to that point?

784: When did you realize that you were 2SLGBTQ+? When did you come out to your friends and family? What was their reaction?

785: Have you ever participated in a Pride parade?

786: How active are you in the community?

787: Were you ever beaten up or bullied for just being yourself?

788: How open are you about your life at work or in general?

789: Would you wanted just to be like anyone else, to blend into the majority or would you prefer to stand out, even if it got you negative attention?

790: Is there anyone in your family/among your friends who is 2SLGBTQ+? Did you always know or find out later? What was your reaction?

791: What, if anything, scares you most about being 2SLGBTQ+?

_____

792: Are you a flirt or are you serious about one partner when you find them?

_____

793: What are your feelings about pronouns?

_____

794: Would you ever help a couple who is 2SLGBTQ+ have children by donating sperm/eggs or being a surrogate? Would you like the child to know you?

_____

It's A Material World

795: Do you have a favorite gemstone? If yes, which type (precious or semi-precious)?

796: Do you have a favorite perfume or cologne? If yes, what is it?

797: What, if any, is your favorite interior design style, e.g. type of furniture, décor?

798: What is your favorite type of vehicle: an SUV, sedan, convertible, minivan, or other?

799: Do you like auctions? Have you been to many? If yes, did you have a winning bid on anything? (What was it?)

800: Is there any type of fabric that you won't wear?

801: If money was no object, what car would you get?

802: If you had to choose between two products, both of which accomplished the same thing, and one was better for the environment but cost more versus the other that cost less but was worse, which would you choose?

803: What is your favorite: hard wood floors, ceramic or tile, or carpeted?

804: Assuming money wasn't an issue, if you bought a house would you prefer one that is in perfect condition with everything done or would you prefer a fixer-upper?

805: If a store or company rips you off or provides a shoddy product or service, how much time and effort are you willing to put in to get satisfaction? Or to at least get revenge?

806: Do you have a favorite plant (not flower or tree)?

807: Do you prefer blinds, curtains, or shutters?

808: What is the strangest thing you have ever bought?

809: Have you ever had your portrait painted?

810: What store have you heard about but never been to and would really like to go to?

_____

811: What would your ideal cottage/ocean front home have?

_____

812: What would be the most extravagant thing you have ever wanted to buy or you think you would want to buy? (In example: a trip around the world in first class)

_____

813: How would you describe your perfect garden? (For example, lots of wildflowers, overgrown, or perfectly trimmed hedges, etc.)

_____

814: How would you describe your perfect bed?

_____

815: Do you ever like to wear hats? If yes, what type and is it important that it be stylish or only important that it be functional?

_____

816: Which do you prefer, wallpaper or paint or pan-elling on walls?

_____

817: What is the best gift you ever remember getting, either as a child or as an adult? (It doesn't have to have been a surprise.)

_____

818: What is the one material thing you don't think you could survive without?

_____

819: What type of chair do you prefer? For example, an armchair or a solid wooden chair or a cushy sofa or something else.

_____

820: If you had a choice of homes, would you prefer an old house or a new house or a high-rise apartment?

_____

821: What was the worst hairstyle or haircut you have ever had?

_____

822: What is your favorite colour for a car?

_____

823: Do you find someone wearing glasses sexy or nerdy or both?

_____

824: If you are dating someone, do you like them to be taller or shorter than you or does it not matter? If it does matter, how much difference in height is ideal to you?

_____

825: What is your favorite type of footwear to wear, for example, running shoes, boots, sandals, etc.?

826: When you are on a first date and are out for a meal, do you prefer to split the bill, have the other person pay, or decide by who invited whom out?

827: Do you love the variety and potential bargains at huge/big box stores, or do you find them grotesque monuments to consumerism?

828: Do you link to pick up trinkets or souvenirs on trips or are they a waste of money?

829: What is the most expensive thing you have ever owned or bought?

830: Do you like to take time and find a bargain or spend more and save time?

831: Would you prefer to get something for free but have to watch ads or to pay for it and not have ads?

832: Do you prefer to buy from smaller, local stores and pay a little more or to get into a car and drive to a big box store to save money? Or do you prefer online shopping?

833: Would you live underground if it was a luxurious home having, for instance, a pool, huge bedrooms, every facility you could thing of?

834: Dishes and laundry: do you let them pile up and be done as needed or they are things that need to be done as soon as possible?

835: Would you boycott a store if you found out the owners had beliefs you considered abhorrent? What if the store offered better deals than competing stores?

836: Would you ever buy a classic car that needed fixing up or would you only want a new vehicle under warranty?

837: Do you spend ages thinking about what to wear on a date or night out (even if you go for a "I just threw this on look") or do you really just throw on whatever is handy?

838: Do you have a magazine, newspaper, or blog you regularly read?

___

839: If you got a personalized license plate — with up to seven letters and numbers — what would you have written on it?

___

840: What have you always wanted but haven't been able to afford?

___

841: Do you like to take free samples when they are offered at stores or events?

___

842: Do you like to assemble IKEA furniture, or do you consider it a task from hell?

___

843: Do you call a professional for home repairs or do you try and fix it yourself?

___

844: Do you know any handicrafts, like knitting or sewing?

___

845: Which do you like better in warm weather, a ceiling fan or air conditioner?

___

846: Have you ever given away something you loved?

_____

847: Is there a colour you would never wear?

_____

848: Do you like dollar stores or do you believe brand names at higher end stores are worth the extra cost?

_____

849: Would you wear a fur coat? What about lambskin or leather coats?

_____

850: Building supply stores: are you a kid in a candy store or a lost tourist looking for directions?

_____

851: Are fashion and style important to you? How would you describe yours?

_____

852: Are you comfortable going into ethnic stores – such as grocery stores – where most of the patrons are speaking a language you don't understand?

_____

853: You inherit some artwork. Among the pieces you find some exquisite antique carvings made from now-illegal materials, such as elephant tusks. Do you destroy them, donate them to a museum, or keep them in your home but out of sight?

_____

854: What is your favorite fabric or material to wear? Least favorite?

_____

855: Is there an item or keepsake that you have always had, such as a gift from your childhood?

_____

856: Do you like to wear a watch? If yes, do you have a favorite brand?

_____

857: If you buy a watch, would you prefer a basic, inexpensive but accurate one or a very expensive and stylish watch (which is also very accurate)?

_____

Food and Drink

858: Do you like peanut butter? If yes, do you prefer smooth or crunchy?

_____

859: favorite chocolate bar?

_____

860: What is your favorite spice?

_____

861: When you were young, what was your favorite type of cereal? How about now?

_____

862: In your orange juice, do you prefer it with pulp or without?

_____

863: favorite type of fruit?

_____

864: Are there any vegetables or fruits that you hate and won't eat?

_____

865: You're on death row and are to be executed the following morning. What would you order as your last meal?

_____

866: What is your favorite type of cheese?

866: _____

867: How do you like having your eggs done best?

_____

868: What is your favorite fast food restaurant?

_____

869: Is there a fruit that you find erotic? If yes, what is it and why?

_____

870: What is your absolute favorite flavour of ice cream or sorbet?

_____

871: What was a favorite food as a child that you don't like now?

_____

872: What are your feelings about Jello?

_____

873: What drink have you heard of that you have never tried but you would like to?

_____

874: What is your favorite type of shooter drink?

_____

875: What is your favorite hot drink and how do you like it served?

_____

876: Hamburgers or hotdogs or wraps?

_____

877: Steak or fish?

_____

878: Would you share your food – for example, french fries – if you were out on a date with someone?

_____

879: What is your favorite vegetable?

_____

880: Is there an everyday sort of food that you can't stand to eat, such as butter or margarine?

_____

881: Are you allergic to anything?

_____

882: What is your favorite snack?

_____

883: If you eat meat, what is the most unusual type of meat you have ever had?

_____

884: What type of food that you hated as a kid do you love now?

_____

885: What type of dessert can you almost never say no to?

_____

886: Coffee, tea, hot chocolate, hot cider: which do you prefer?

_____

887: Do you like farmers' markets or buying vegetables from a stand in country?

_____

888: What is your favorite candy?

_____

889: Do you prefer a small, intimate restaurant or a loud, crowded club or bar?

_____

890: Do you have a favorite type of sandwich? What condiments do you like on it?

_____

891: What is your favorite type of bread?

_____

892: Do you have a favorite type of soup?

_____

893: Do you have a favorite type of pasta?

_____

894: Do you like spicy food or sauces?

_____

895: Do you prefer fast food or a simple meal to save time or do you prefer a more elaborate meal that may take longer to prepare and be better for you?

896: Vitamin pills: good as a health supplement or complete scam and waste of money?

897: If you are vegan, are you comfortable dating someone who isn't or if you are a meat-eater, could you date a vegan?

898: Have you ever been out at a restaurant and sent your meal back to the kitchen because there was something wrong with it?

899: What is the weirdest drink you have ever had?

900: Do you have a favorite type of cookie?

901: Is there a table habit – such as slurping soup – that particularly annoys you?

902: What is the most disgusting thing you have ever had to eat?

903: Do you like to try new foods, or do you prefer to stay in your comfort zone?

_____

904: What toppings does your ideal pizza have?

_____

905: If you drink coffee, do you have a favorite type or style of coffee?

_____

906: If you drink tea, do you have a favorite blend?

_____

Kind of Nerdy

907: If you could have any superpower, what would it be and why would you choose it? Would you punish those who you believe have wronged you in the past?

908: If you could become any animal or creature, which would you choose and why?

909: If you were cursed to become a creature, such as a vampire, zombie, werewolf, or a ghost or something like that, and you could choose, which would you go for and why?

910: How comfortable are you with new technology or gadgets, like smart speakers?

911: Imagine a world with no electricity. What would you choose to do as your occupation? (Assumes basics like food are met.)

912: If you were allowed to name a city or town, what would you call it?

913: Do you have a favorite superhero? Super villain?

914: Who do you consider to be the greatest villain in history?

_____

915: If there was some sort of apocalypse, such as a plague, would you want to survive? If yes, what would you be willing to do to survive?

_____

916: If you heard a place was haunted, would you want to investigate or stay as far away as you could?

_____

917: Are you a city mouse or a country mouse?

_____

918: How do you feel about social media, like Facebook, Instagram, Snapchat, etc.?

_____

919: Do you like board games or games like chess or checkers?

_____

920: If your loved ones turned into zombies – with no hope of ever being cured – would you be able to kill them?

_____

921: Is there anyone you follow online that you don't personally know?

_____

922: Have you ever bought any type of cryptocurrency, like bitcoin?

923: Have you ever played video/computer games or eSport/MMO games? If yes, which ones and why those ones?

924: Do you see a new device as something to get excited about or something to conquer?

925: Which do you prefer to use if you need to go on the internet: a laptop/computer, a tablet, or a smartphone?

926: You get one wish and no more: what do you wish for?

927: What is your perception of the universe?

928: How much do you know? Is it enough or do you want to know more?

929: Is there a device – like a DVD player – that isn't being used or as common as before that you miss?

930: Do you have a favorite type font?

931: If you had to choose between ghosts and angels, which one would you want to exist?

___

932: What do you think when someone starts to tell you about a conspiracy theory they believe in?

___

933: Bookstores and libraries: relics from a bygone age or temples of knowledge?

___

934: Star Wars or Star Trek or the Harry Potter movies: which is the best?

___

935: Who would win in a fight between Superman and Captain Marvel? (Don't even talk about Batman – he isn't in the same league.)

___

936: Who is your favorite Doctor Who? Do you have a favorite companion of the Doctor?

___

937: Have you ever played a role-playing game like Dungeons & Dragons?

___

938: Comic books/graphic novels: a genius marriage of illustration and writing or a sign that the illiterate fanboys have taken over publishing?

___

939: If you could invent something, what would you invent?

___

940: What is the most fanboy/fangirl thing you have done?

___

941: Is there a myth that you think might be true or that has a strong basis in reality, such as King Arthur?

___

942: If you had to choose a natural disaster to be caught up in, which would you choose?

___

943: According to Socrates the unexamined life is not worth living. Is this worth considering or just nonsense from a long-dead Greek guy?

___

944: As a child, which mythological creature did you like best, if any? For example: mermaids or gnomes.

___

945: What stories scared you the most as a child? What stories did you like the best?

___

946: What movie scared you so much that it still frightens you?

___

947: Are you the hero of the story of your life or the villain?

_____

948: Do you like to watch YouTube or other online videos to learn how to do new things?

_____

949: Do you ever google people after you meet them?

_____

950: How do you feel about science fiction stories, movies, or tv? Do you have a favorite?

_____

Potpourri of Curiosity

951: What was your favorite moment over the past weekend?

_____

952: What do you think about royalty?

_____

953: Do you have a favorite type of cloud?

_____

954: If something was named after you or dedicated to you (i.e., a song, book, street, town, ship etc.,), what would you most like it to be?

_____

955: If you could bring back one extinct creature, what would it be?

_____

956: What is your favorite day of the week?

_____

957: Would you sing on a crowded subway if you felt like singing?

_____

958: Is there a word that you have always thought was a strange one? For example, artichoke?

_____

959: What is the worst thing you have ever smelled?

_____

960: Do you prefer lions or tigers?

_____

961: Do you prefer to watch the wind in the leaves or the ripples in the water?

_____

962: Lately the world has seen the rise of more populists. Do you think this is due to the world needing strong leaders or due to people desiring simple answers to complex questions?

_____

963: If someone you didn't know randomly came up to you on a crowded street, gave you a flower, and walked away, what would you think?

_____

964: Did you ever decide you needed to reveal a big secret to your family? How did they react if you went ahead?

_____

965: How do you feel about surveys? Choose one of the following: A: Give me more. B: Meh C: Next question, please.

_____

966: Do people committing infractions but causing no harm, upset you or do you just let it slide?

_____

967: When the door of life says "Push", do you try and pull?

_____

968: What word, whenever you hear it, makes you laugh or smile? What word truly offends you?

_____

969: Freckles: cute as a button or mark of the devil?

_____

970: What is the biggest mistaken assumption you have ever made?

_____

971: Have you ever found a significant amount of money by accident – i.e., laying on the sidewalk or in an old book you bought?

_____

972: Would you ever donate an organ or tissue to a stranger? What about a relative?

_____

973: Are you an early bird or a night owl?

_____

974: Do you know how to make any shadow puppets?

_____

975: Trampolines: most fun you can have standing up or insane death traps waiting to snap up children?

976: Would you describe yourself as having any level of paranoia? Be honest. People are watching.

977: Do you think life is a comedy or a tragedy?

978: An insect is crawling near you but poses no threat: do you kill it, capture it to release outside, or ignore it?

979: If good fences make good neighbours, do you believe in physical and mental fences between yourself and people around you?

980: Have you ever written any poetry? If yes, did you share it with anyone?

981: What really annoys you? Huh, huh? Come on, tell me.

982: Have you ever hunted for four-leaf clovers?

983: Have you ever had an unusual pet, such as a rat or a tarantula?

984: What is the strangest nickname you have ever heard for someone you met?

_____

985: Do you have a favorite joke? If yes, can you tell me it?

_____

986: How do you feel about having to iron your clothing?

_____

987: How do people describe your handwriting? How do you describe it? Is good handwriting important to you?

_____

988: Did you work on your signature until you liked it or did you just let it happen?

_____

989: If you could save one species from going extinct, which would it be?

_____

990: Do you throw coins into wishing wells or fountains?

_____

991: Have you ever used a fire extinguisher in a real emergency? Have you ever pulled or activated a fire alarm?

_____

992: If you ran into an old friend and they asked "What happened to you?", how would you answer?

_____

993: Have you ever destroyed a book on purpose?

_____

994: Do you have a secret indulgence?

_____

995: Is this country the greatest country in the history of the world? Why?

_____

996: What are you most curious to try?

_____

997: You hear a child crying near you in a public place, like a store: do you check to see they are ok or are you confident that the child's parents will look after them?

_____

998: What would you be willing to do to help stop or slow down climate change?

_____

999: What, if anything, scares or concerns you most about climate change?

_____

One Last Question

(If it is the right time and place to ask.)

1000: Will you marry me? Or should I ask you some more questions?

_____

Maybe it isn't the right time to ask. Or they need some time to think. So, here are a couple of fluffy questions in the meantime.

Extra #1: What is the cutest: toddlers, puppies, or kittens?

_____

Extra #2: Have you ever been to an event that had name tags and forgotten to take the name tag off afterwards?

_____

Good luck and I hope your questioning has brought knowledge and happiness.

About the Author

Christopher Eyton

Born in Toronto, Canada and a fervent asker of questions, Christopher Eyton studied history at the University of King's College, Halifax. Travelled. He got married, had two amazing children whom he doesn't see as often as he would like. (They are millenials with their own lives - such is life.) Got divorced. Travelled some more. Dated. Found some more happiness and learned to love kdrama and kpop. Keeps asking questions and has no intentions of stopping. Getting older and trying to figure that out.

Email: christophereyton@gmail.com

Instragram: @cmeyton

Photography: christophereyton.picfair.com

Find my other books on Amazon.